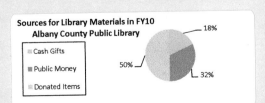

Sources for Library Materials in FY10
Albany County Public Library

- Cash Gifts
- Public Money
- Donated Items

18%

50%

32%

MY HAVANA

First edition 2010

Library of Congress Cataloging-in-Publication Data

Wells, Rosemary.
My Havana : memories of a Cuban boyhood/ Rosemary Wells with Secundino Fernandez ;
illustrated by Peter Ferguson. — 1st ed.
p. cm.
Summary: Relates events in the childhood of architect Secundino Fernandez, who left his beloved
Havana, Cuba, with his parents, first to spend a year in Spain, and later to move to New York City.

ISBN 978-0-7636-4305-8

1. Fernandez, Secundino — Childhood and youth — Juvenile fiction.
[1. Fernandez, Secundino — Childhood and youth — Fiction. 2. Havana (Cuba) — History —
20th century — Fiction. 3. Cuba — History — 20th century — Fiction.
4. Architecture — Fiction. 5. Family life — Cuba — Fiction. 6. Dictators — Fiction.]
I. Fernandez, Secundino. II. Ferguson, Peter, date. ill. III. Title.
PZ7.W46843Mxt 2010
[Fic] — dc22   2009012053

10 11 12 13 14 15 LEO 10 9 8 7 6 5 4 3 2 1

Printed in Heshan, Guangdong, China

This book was typeset in OPTILuciusAd.
The illustrations were done in oil and pencil.

Candlewick Press
99 Dover Street
Somerville, Massachusetts 02144

visit us at www.candlewick.com

MY HAVANA

ROSEMARY WELLS

with SECUNDINO FERNANDEZ

illustrated by PETER FERGUSON

CANDLEWICK PRESS

Dino Fernandez, age 8, with his parents

Dino Fernandez, age 10

"People will believe anything," says my father.

We are watching our six-inch black-and-white television. It is 1959. I am eleven. On the screen, a man is yelling. The jabbing of his finger reminds me of a man arguing with his mother.

"Fidel is a rich man's son, Dino," Papi whispers to me. "He went to the best private school in Havana, but he's trying to look like a poor peasant! Everyone thinks he is Robin Hood sent from heaven to save Cuba. He calls himself *El Líder*."

This leader does not shave his neck like a gentleman. His mustache curls around his lips. His beard grows up out of his collar like wild moss on a palm tree.

My father's hand rests on my shoulder. "He will be another dictator, much worse than the last one," he says.

HAVANA
1952–1954

Until I am six years old, in 1954, my world is sweet. "We live in a city built by angels," Papi says. There is no cold in Havana, only sunshine and warm rain. The city's avenues are lined with arcades of coral-stone archways, ancient doors, and window frames painted bright as birds-of-paradise. The vivid colors are accented everywhere by the deep mahogany of Havana's window shutters and ceiling fans.

From the time I am four, I am taught at Saint Augustine's, a school run by gentle priests at the Plaza del Cristo, in downtown Havana. After school I come home to our apartment above my *papi* and *mami's* restaurant on Virtudes Street. Every day I walk with my best friend, Alfonso, across the Parque Central and see the towering capitol to my left. Every evening my mother fills a porcelain dish with *pasteles* to fatten me up. I, Dino Fernandez, am very small. I wear glasses and don't ever finish my supper plate.

"You are your *mami*'s little *pastel!*" Alfonso always says.

Alfonso is sure that I will grow up to be a fussy old professor with white hair growing out of my nose. I am positive Alfonso will play on one of Cuba's national baseball teams.

Our favorite walk home is down the Prado and on to the Malecón, the curved sea wall along the shoreline facing Morro Castle. During storms the seawater smashes across the road, and we run into the waves right on the street. Some days Alfonso and I walk down the Avenida de las Misiones, which is lined with tall palm trees and passes by the palace that long ago belonged to the president of Cuba. El Palacio Presidencial is built of fine coral stone, marble, and rare hardwoods. Alfonso dribbles his ball from foot to foot. I catch his spinning ball in the crook of my ankle, but my heart is in the mysterious stairs and doorways of el Palacio Presidencial.

"You are always wasting time looking up at buildings, Dino!" whines Alfonso. He hates it when

I come to a sudden stop in the street and sketch a building all over the pages of my religion homework.

For luck I run up and touch the marble column at the entrance to *el palacio*. Long ago, my grandfather Marcelino built another Cuban president's house with his own hands. When I lay my finger on the stone column, I touch a little of him.

All I know of my grandparents Abuelo Marcelino and Abuela Maria is that they lived in Cuba for many years and raised their children here. Then suddenly, long before I was born, they sailed back to their native Spain. Just why they did is one of those grown-up stories, half told and half not. Grown-ups don't explain. Like raindrops on a window, their words just slide away.

My mother did not go to Spain with her parents. She was old enough by then to stay in Havana and find work. She took a job as a maid in the Roosevelt Hotel. My father was the headwaiter. Mami and Papi had five dollars between them on their wedding day. Papi started a little restaurant on Zulueta Street, and a few years later they had me.

* * *

I begin to draw buildings when I am just able to hold a pencil.

My cousins say, "Dino has a screw loose — filling all those silly sketchbooks with windows and doorways!"

I wouldn't dare tell my teasing cousins that Havana is like another mother to me, dressed in beautiful colors with sparkling jewelry.

So I tell only my favorite cousin, Mercy. Mercy never makes fun of my sketchbooks. She helps me cut out my drawings carefully, following the lines of the roofs and walls. We string the pictures together with Scotch tape, make a circle of the drawn buildings, and sit inside the ring.

Downtown, Papi takes me shopping. Sometimes we go to the cheap food vendors, sometimes to the expensive Galiano shops. Havana's old buildings have doorways three times the height of a good-size man. I can never get enough of these doorways. What secret courtyards lie beyond the huge mahogany doors with brass handles?

On our street, I try to see into people's windows and behind the lazy blowing curtains. Havana windows can be nearly as tall as the doorways. "Do not stare at people through the window!" Papi tells me. "It is rude, Dino."

I pay no attention. When I am alone in the street, I peer in at women pouring coffee, men in undershirts, dogs curled on sofas. On some old Havana houses, lizards crawl right out of the holes in the stone and change color with the light. Tiny palm sprouts and flowers take hold everywhere, pushing right out of the buildings themselves, crumbling the weak plaster with their strong roots.

"You are always stopping, Dino," Papi says, laughing. I stare at the miracle beneath my feet: eight-sided red tiles, swept and polished to a buttery glow each morning by the shop owners.

Papi waits while I memorize the fiery blue of a stained-glass window. He lights a cigar and reads his paper. Deep in the shade of an archway, I test the chill of the night-cooled stone and compare it to the blistering heat of the street.

At twilight Alfonso and I are allowed to wander Old Havana's alleyways, among banana sellers and domino players, sailors with their girls, and women hanging laundry. Entire families, great-grandpa to baby, sit outside on the winding streets eating at tables set on the paving stones and playing checkers with the neighbors at the day's end. Havana is all the colors of a peach. Papi calls it the "Paris of the Americas." To me it is the Paris of my heart.

Some days Mami takes me down to the harbor. She points out the ships that come in from Spain. "La Coruña," she says. "Madrid. Three thousand miles away, Dino." Tears creep into her voice. "Abuela and Abuelo have never met your *papi*, have never seen their grandson."

Then one day my father receives a telegram from Spain. Papi's older brother, José, has fallen from a rooftop where he was making repairs. José has a wife and eight young children at home.

"We must help José's family," says my father. Papi places our restaurant in the hands of his chef, Pepe. Mami is thrilled that we are going to Spain.

MADRID

1954–1956

We pack our bags. We board a steamship with two orange funnels. It is October 1954.

All the way to Spain, I am seasick and lie in my bunk. Papi and Mami place teaspoons of *crème de menthe* to my lips. I clench my teeth shut against the horrible green liquid that is meant to cure seasickness but only makes it worse.

At the port of La Coruña, Abuelo Marcelino and Abuela Maria wait for us in an old rowboat in the middle of the harbor, where they can watch our big ship arrive and dock. My *abuela*, Maria de la Remedios Sanchez Pascual, now an old woman, stands up in the little boat, as tall as the queen on a chessboard.

"See?" Mami shouts. "There they are!"

I wave my Cuban flag to them, and they see me.

Mami shouts again, louder, "Oh, don't row too close to our huge ship, Papi! Don't stand up, Mami! It is too dangerous!"

Their little boat steadies. Abuelo makes Abuela sit and rows off toward the docks.

The air smells of iron and salt. Shrieking gulls wheel around the gunnels of our ship, looking for food. They fly so near that I think they will land on my head with their flat yellow feet. Beyond the wharf is a row of gray buildings. Against the gray sky are dust-brown hills. I feel crisp October air for the first time in my life. Our ship shudders, and a loudspeaker tells us to assemble at the gangway. When we get off the boat with all our bags and satchels, we are told to go to the customs police.

These policemen do not smile like Cuban ones. They wear shiny black helmets in the shape of bats. All passengers are inspected in the customs shed. Our bags are stuffed with nylon stockings, coffee, and bags of sugar for our families. The customs police help themselves to some of it when my father is not looking. "Stop!" I say to them. "That's not yours to take!"

A lady in a stiff dark uniform marches me away from my parents. "Strip, boy!" she orders, and begins to unbutton my shirt with white rubber-gloved hands. "When people have something to hide," she huffs, "they tape it to their children's bodies!"

I must take off all my clothing so that she can see whether I have anything forbidden taped to my body. What is she looking for? What kind of country is this? The customs lady wears men's shoes. Her uniform stinks of cigarette smoke and indoor office sweat. I begin to cry and shake from the cold.

She stamps her foot. "Stop that crying! Are you nothing but a baby in diapers?"

My mother puts her finger to her lips.

The customs officer watches as I throw my clothing back on, but after ten days on a rolling ship, I am not used to the steadiness of dry land. I fall backward clumsily.

"He'll find out that Spanish boys have more spine than that!" she says to my mother with a sniff. My mother's hands tremble as she guides me from the building. Outdoors at last, I breathe hard to get the stink out of my nose.

"I am scared of the police!" I tell Papi.

"I am scared of them, too, Dino," he says.

"But, Papi, why are they so mean?"

This is his answer: "Spain is ruled by an old man whom no one elected. His name is Generalissimo Francisco Franco. These are Franco's soldiers, left over from a long-ago war. They learned how to be cruel in that war."

"Is Franco a bad man, Papi?" I ask.

My father nods and winks. "An old tarantula," he says. "A dictator." But he does not explain what a dictator is.

We go by railway to Madrid. Abuela Maria and Abuelo Marcelino give me sticky rock candy. They pass me back and forth as if I am a prize just delivered to them. I stare at their eyes and hair, teeth and noses, and see my mother divided into two people.

The train jerks and joggles so that no one can stand up without falling. It smells of tobacco and urine. The wooden seats are stained. Under them are a dozen cigarette ends, unswept.

"I think a dog has gone pee-pee in this car!" says Mami.

"This train is an old one," Abuela and Abuelo explain apologetically.

After we leave the mountains behind, the dryness of Spain's Castile region blows through the window. We pass little chalky towns one after the other that spill by us in the brown hills. Dust stings my eyes. I listen to the Spanish of my grandparents. It is smoother than Cuban. Papi says I am to go to school here. Does that mean I will have to speak that way?

* * *

My first day in Madrid, I try to draw the buildings.
But the drawings do not come. High up in the tall
apartments, people close their dusky yellow shutters
to the outside world. The windows are solemn, like
eyes that won't look at you. No one plays dominos
or eats supper in the street. There are no trees in the
Madrid parks, no trees even in the mountains all
around.

"In the war years," Abuela Maria explains, "we
burned all the trees in woodstoves to keep warm and
to cook our dinners. "

Papi leaves us to help his brother's family in the
north of Spain. It is decided that I will stay in
Madrid with Mami. After a few days, Mami notices
my empty sketchbook. She sits me down and combs
back my hair. She asks, "What is wrong, Dino? You
are not drawing! There are many beautiful palaces
and arcades here in Madrid."

I try to explain. Madrid is a brown and gray city.

There is no ocean, and no palm trees or flowers growing out of the mortar in the bricks.

"But Madrid is a great capital city all the same. It has many famous cathedrals and museums," says Mami to encourage me.

"At home," I tell her, "people smile and say hello to me and Alfonso. Here, they look at me as if I might steal something."

I can see from her eyes that she agrees with me. "It's not so friendly as home," she says. "The old Madrid families and Franco, the dictator, rule life here with an iron hand."

There is that word again. "What is that? *Dictator?*" I ask her.

She lowers her voice. "All is ordered by the dictator. Everyone is afraid of his police. People don't laugh and play freely in the streets the way they do at home. A dictator rules like the kings in olden days, Dino. The rules are whatever he feels like making them, and can change at any time. No one can unelect him. He will be there until he dies."

"Who is this Franco?" I ask.

"Some people say he was a friend of Hitler," says Mami, still in a whisper. Her eyes look one way and then the other, as if someone might overhear.

Back home, the *padres* at Saint Augustine's had taught us that Hitler was a madman who killed ten million people. How could someone like Hitler have an old friend?

Papi has been at Tío José's in the village of Burón, caring for José's family for three weeks when Mami goes north to help, too. They do not tell me when we will return to Cuba. They leave me with Abuela and Abuelo, and I enter the local boys' academy. I am afraid we will never go home again.

"You miss your *mami* and *papi*," says Abuelo.

"And my home," I say.

Abuela buys eggs and butter in secret from a man who hides them under his cloak and comes to the back door at night. Almost nothing from the outside, goods or medicine, ever makes its way into Francisco Franco's Spain. "Franco makes himself and his friends rich," says Abuela Maria, "while the rest of

us live on bread and water." She says this very softly, as if someone might be hiding, listening.

Abuelo Marcelino shows me how to sand and oil wood until it is as soft as a kitten's skin. I take his huge, hard hands in my small, soft ones. Under the whorls of his palms lie hard calluses like something seen under the surface of water.

"Someday I'll have hands like yours," I tell him.

"Someday, Dino, you will work with your head, not with your hands," Abuelo tells me. There is heat in his voice, and fire in his old eyes.

"Is that better?" I ask him.

"No," he tells me. "It is holy to work with your hands, Dino. But carpenters are paid nothing. Men who work with their heads have soft beds and beefsteak."

Each morning in school we must salute the picture of Generalissimo Franco. He looks like a very old rabbit to me. We sing the Spanish national anthem and recite an oath  of allegiance. But I don't say the oath of allegiance. Instead, barely moving my lips, I say, "I am Cuban, not Spanish. You cannot hurt me, old rabbit-face."

The boys in my Madrid grammar school laugh at my Havana accent. They call me "Cuba." "Kooba! Kooba! Kooba!" By the third day of classes, I begin to say *"th"* instead of *"es"* to sound like the Spanish boys.

Abuela finds me in bed drawing one night. She takes my sketchbook and turns it so that she can see the pictures. "These are not Madrid buildings, Dino," she says. "These are Havana buildings."

"I have a stone where my stomach is," I tell her, pointing to my belly.

She places a dry, cool hand on my forehead and says, "You are homesick, my precious boy. One day you will go back — just hold on." She puts my good-night milk on the side table and turns out the light. Abuela has paid a small fortune for the milk even though I saw the milkman add water to it when she wasn't watching. When Mami comes back, she fills the money jar in the kitchen with silver coins. She does this when Abuela is not looking.

Another year passes, and I think we will be stuck in Madrid forever when a telegram arrives from Havana. It is from Pepe. He can no longer manage Papi's restaurant alone. Luckily, Tío José can now walk without crutches. He is ready to go back to work.

Before we sail home, Abuela and Abuelo take me to visit José's family in Burón. On the north coast of Spain, I smell the sea for the first time in two years, and it lightens my heart. The sunlight is different there.

In the week before our boat sails back to Cuba, I begin to draw Spain. I sketch the Roman wall that surrounds the city of Lugo. Both wall and city were

built before the time of Christ. Everything, even the stone, sags a little because it is so ancient. There are miles of crumbling wall and an old ruined castle. The houses, built of softly colored ancient stones, lean against one another like sleeping dogs. I draw from early morning to evening.

My Spanish cousins are all fair and blue-eyed like Papi, like me. Papi tells me that thousands of years ago, this part of Spain, Galicia, was settled by the ancestors of the Irish. There is an old man down the street who knows how to play the bagpipes. I draw him, too, beside the wall where he sits in the sun.

"Why are you drawing the wall?" my cousins ask. "The wall is old and boring. Why don't you draw cars and motorcycles? Those are cool."

I fill a whole sketchbook with the wall. Laid end to end and Scotch-taped together, those pages make a small wall themselves, but I don't show it to my cousins.

HOME
1956-1959

On my first day back in Havana, my eyes almost hurt from so much bright color. I wander the streets with my head up like a tourist. "I will never leave you again," I whisper to my city.

Alfonso waits for me on the front steps of Saint Augustine's School on the Plaza del Cristo. As if I had never left, he passes me his soccer ball and I catch it in the crook of my ankle.

"You talk like a *gallego,* Dino," says Alfonso. I bite my tongue and drop my carefully practiced Madrid lisp, changing *"th"* back to *"es."*

As if to catch up, I draw pictures of the Edificio Bacardí. It is my favorite of all the Havana palaces. My hand draws more quickly now, and I use colored pencils with greater deftness.

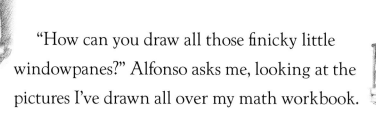

"How can you draw all those finicky little windowpanes?" Alfonso asks me, looking at the pictures I've drawn all over my math workbook.

I answer him. "Easy! I could draw the whole city and never stop until I had every building on paper!"

Once in a while, the president of Cuba, General Fulgencio Batista, and his followers come to eat at my father's restaurant. Mami never sends a bill to their table.

"Send over their check, please, Pilar," Papi insists to my mother. "They can pay the tab like everyone else, the fat sons of a sow!"

But my mother is careful. "Don't ask for trouble!" she says, and allows Batista and his friends to eat and drink for nothing.

"Oh, Batista!" says Alfonso when I ask him why my parents are so afraid of *el presidente.* "He's friends with all the Mafia crooks. You know that Batista just took over as *presidente* one day, don't you? Kicked the last one out. Batista's a regular dictator."

Is this Batista, this dictator, another friend of Hitler?

 I see no police in black bat hats, and there is no saluting Batista's picture at Saint Augustine's School.

Then one day I find Mami crying in her bedroom.

"What is it, Mami?" I ask.

She takes a deep breath. "You are old enough to know, Dino," she says, blowing her nose. "Everything is not fine."

"What happened?"

"Last night when the kitchen was closed and you were fast asleep, Batista's police chief came in. He wants Papi to go into a line of business owned by gangsters."

"What did Papi say?"

"He said that that kind of business was disgraceful, and he refused. But now Papi is nervous about being on the wrong side of Batista's police. I am afraid they might arrest him and close the restaurant because they are angry with him."

* * *

In the middle of the night on New Year's Eve, 1958, Batista is chased out of Cuba by Fidel Castro, the shouting man in army fatigues and a peasant's beard. In the morning I hear people screaming up and down the streets. Over breakfast, Papi tells me what happened. He does not look happy.

"Aren't you happy, Papi?" I ask. "The dictator is gone. Won't our restaurant be safe now, with the shouting man as *presidente*?"

"Fidel's *compadre* Che Guevara promises that all rents in Cuba will be reduced, all wages increased," Papi says. "Everything in Cuba will be evenly divided and given to the people. No rich, no poor, everyone the same. Cuba will be like heaven on earth. What nonsense!"

One night very late, I come down to the restaurant from bed because I cannot sleep. I curl up under an unused corner table so that the voices of the customers can lull me to sleep.

But the chairs are pulled out. Sitting down are Mercy's parents, my uncle Bernardo and my aunt

Amelia. Bernardo is very upset. Tears run down my auntie's cheeks. My whole body tenses. I know I may hear secrets that I am not meant to hear. Papi arrives. Then Mami.

Tío Bernardo says to Papi, "This Che Guevara fellow, he came to my office yesterday. He told me I must give over my company, my house, and all my money to the army of the people. What could I do?" Bernardo asks. He points to the temple of his head with his finger imitating a pistol. "He held a gun to my head. He told me I will be lucky to escape with my life. I have worked my hands to the bone for twenty years to set up my little company. The way you have in this restaurant, Secundino!"

"This Che," sniffs Amelia. "He is the darling of the world, like a movie star. His eyelashes are so long, men as well as women fall over him in love! He is not even Cuban. He is a ———." Here Tía Amelia uses a bad word in Cuban for *Argentinian.*

When they leave, I crawl upstairs and shake with chills in my bed, not falling asleep until dawn.

New York
1959–

On a sleepy Thursday afternoon, *El Líder*'s soldiers shoot a man one block from my school. We do not know why. All of us boys are let out early, and our mothers race to the school to take us home.

"Mami, I am not afraid!" I say.

"Well, I am," she says.

"Will he take your restaurant away, Papi?" I ask. "What will we do?"

"I don't mean to wait around and see," Papi says. "We will go and help Tío Manuel run his store in New York City. In the early morning, there is a plane for Miami."

My big father folds my small mother into his coat. His arms surround her like walls. When she stops crying, she trembles, and when she stops shaking, she begins to cry again.

"Dino should pack his things," says my father.

"What good is that?" asks my mother. "Everything he owns is for Cuba. New York is freezing, like the meat locker in the butcher shop."

I picture that meat locker. Whenever the butcher opens its door, a fog pours out from where the secret beefs and porks hang. Was New York like that?

"I want to go out," I say to my father.

"No, it is too dangerous, Dino," he says.

"But I want to say good-bye," I complain.

"You may write letters to Father Pacitto and to Mercy and to Alfonso. Give the letters to Pepe, Dino. He will deliver them when we are safely gone."

But it was not Father Pacitto, Mercy, or Alfonso I was thinking of. I wanted to say good-bye to the Edificio Bacardí, to the building's goddesses holding vases of glass jewels, malachite, and gold. I wanted to stand in the shadow of the Palacio de los Condes de Jaruco, with its delicate columns and archways, its cobalt-blue balconies and stained-glass windows. I wanted to listen one last time to the wind in the palms that circled the harbor facing El Palacio Presidencial.

I wanted to say good-bye to the little
Café Loro Azul, the Blue Parrot Café,
where sailors from the boats and women
in sequined dresses went. My mother and
father would never go into this sailors' café. But
its blue neon light in the shape of a parrot flickered
all night long, and the music spilled across the
cobblestones of the Avenida del Puerto. I held that
neon parrot as close to me as I was supposed to hold
the religious medal that hung around my neck.

In Miami we board the Silver Meteor train bound
for New York. I have the window seat.

"Eat your sandwich, Dino," says my father.

I push it away. I have never tasted anything like
the cottony Wonder bread or rubbery American
cheese in my life.

"I would like a Cuban sandwich, please, Papi. I
can't eat this," I say.

"Tomorrow we will be in New York," says my
mother. "And Tío Manuel will feed you a good
supper."

"In the meantime," adds my father, "you must eat something, Dino. Think of it this way: American bread *is* a disaster. But on the other hand, there are no dictators here. No Francos, Batistas, or *El Líders*."

"Who do the Americans have?" I ask.

"A man called Eisenhower," says my father. "He is honest and fair. Now go to sleep, Dino."

In the morning the landscape has changed from green, sunny Florida to brown, icy New Jersey.

"The trees have no leaves!" I say, startled out of my sleepiness.

My father passes me a cup of coffee, heavy with cream and sugar.

"They will come back green in spring," says my father.

Then we dive into the sudden blackness of a tunnel. Across the seats, two American girls chatter in English. They don't speak in the simple English language sentences I learned from Father Ramón at Saint Augustine's. There's no "Hello! How. Are. You. Today? My. Name. Is. Dino." I can't understand a word they say.

We step out onto the sidewalk at New York City's Penn Station and get in line for a taxicab. Icy wind blows up my cotton trouser legs. "What is that falling from the sky?" I ask Papi.

Papi has been in New York before. "It is called sleet," he says, using the English word. There is no word for sleet in Cuban.

New York is a terribly black and gray city. The weak, white sunshine has no more warmth than a candle. Like in Madrid, not a tree grows on New York's streets. No one here in the land of ice could bring a table outside to play dominos. I note things to write to Alfonso later. "When you fall and scrape your skin on pavement," I want to tell him, "that is how New York feels against the eye."

* * *

My *tío* Manuel takes me to Barneys boys shop for wool suits and a winter coat. He brings me to school, P.S. 3, at Hudson and Grove Streets. He tells me what number bus to catch home when school is over.

Mrs. Mary Brown frowns at me when I enter her fourth-grade class, holding the note from the principal and trying to smile.

"Can't you talk, young man?" she asks after reading the note.

I shake my head.

"Go back to the office, then," she says. "You certainly can't be in my class!"

I don't understand.

A girl in the first row whispers to me in a fierce kind of Spanish that I have never heard. "*Vamos!*" she hisses.

Three times the office sends me back to Mrs. Brown's class. Three times she sends me back to the office. I rattle down the wooden hallways of the school, nearly throwing up in fear of Mrs. Brown.

Finally, she allows me to stay, but she will not look at me.

At the end of the day, the right number bus does not come. I walk. Soon I am lost and coughing, the air full of coal soot and car exhaust. It is dark when I find my way to Eighth Avenue and Fourteenth Street.

"I had no lunch," I say to Mami, dropping my books on the floor. "I didn't know the word for lunch. I couldn't find the right bus home."

Mami has made roast pork with fried bananas—a house specialty at our restaurant—and she feeds me the best slices.

It is not a good beginning. My Spanish-speaking classmates are no help at all. They are from the island of Puerto Rico and speak a different kind of Spanish. They do not believe for one minute that I, with my blue eyes and freckled face, am anything like them.

My English teacher, Miss Neubold, asks for book reports. I panic. Tío Manuel writes one for me on Charles Dickens's four-hundred-page novel *A Tale of Two Cities*.

"You," says Miss Neubold the next day, pointing her finger at me, "can't even read the *Daily News,* much less Charles Dickens!" She sends me down to the kindergarten for the rest of the day. I am too embarrassed to cry in front of the five-year-olds.

Then I begin to draw maps for Miss Neubold to illustrate a real book report. Miss Neubold likes my maps. She brings me back to my seat in fourth grade.

January and February roar up and down New York City's avenues. There is no going out in New York twilight as there was in our neighborhood in Havana. Night comes early. It drops across the city like a black curtain. My father puts a small American flag over my bed alongside my Cuban one. I take it down. "I want to go home," I say.

"Dino," says Papi, "this time we cannot go home. Havana is in the hands of madmen. New York is our home now."

I block my ears at his words. I hate the cold. I hate this dreary, black city. I hate this terrible English language, with its weird spelling and ungentle words.

After supper I look out my window; I squint and pretend I see the lights of Havana. But there is no flickering blue parrot sign at the Café Loro Azul. Homesickness sweeps over me.

But in the way that a fallen bird struggles to fly again, I begin to build. I lay a large piece of plywood on my bedroom floor. On it I paint the map of Havana showing its main *avenidas*. I put the Castillo del Morro right at the entrance to the harbor. I trace the Malecón by the water where Alfonso and I used to walk. The harbor itself I make out of aluminum foil glued to the board and glazed with blue nail varnish.

With great care I cut my favorite buildings out of cardboard. I paint archways and balconies, drawn to scale with a ruler, compass, and pen. Streets large and small spider out across the floor of my bedroom. One night I make the capitol, another night the Roosevelt Hotel in honor of my parents' first meeting. The Café Loro Azul, its neon parrot in blue and silver ink, takes its place on the Calle San Lázaro.

I paint with all the bright colors of Havana. With fluorescent paint I fill each window and streetlight, and every porthole of the ships in the harbor. When I turn out the bedside lamp, my Havana sparkles and shines like the real thing. From my bedroom floor, I believe I can hear dance music pouring out from the Café Loro Azul. Distant Cuban melodies suspend me above the mysterious lights. And this Havana, city of memory, saves me from the homesickness. Sleep usually overtakes me before the phosphorous paint fades in the darkness. I slide my Havana under my bed and go to sleep.

One day in February, Mami asks me to translate a note from our neighbor. I read the English easily.

"You can speak English, Dino!" she says. "You understand."

It is true. I've learned it from the radio, from the ads in the subway, from the other kids, and especially from the boy who sits behind me in class, John Mitovikios. "Show me how you draw those maps!"

he whispered when he saw one of my illustrated book reports. After that, I asked him to come to our house, and I showed him how to make maps at our kitchen table with crow-quill pens and colored pencils.

"We are going to Coney Island on Saturday," Tío Manuel announces one day in May. "You may bring a friend, Dino."

I ask John Mitovikios to come along.

Primavera is the Spanish word for springtime. In New York, springtime is everything. John is becoming my best friend, I am speaking English, and Mrs. Brown has promoted me to the fifth grade.

Tío Manuel takes John and me on the subway for over an hour to Brooklyn. At the top of the subway steps is a very different New York. Everywhere people are eating fried clams and hot dogs at outdoor tables. Old men play checkers and dominos. Seagulls land near the children, who throw torn bread and cheer when the gulls catch the crumbs in the air.

Holding our hands, Tío Manuel walks us down the splintery boardwalk. We shoot rubber ducks with BB guns and have our fortunes told. Tío Manuel lets us go up the Parachute Jump by ourselves.

"It is too much for my heart," Tío Manuel says.

At the very top of the ride, before we plunge down in a free fall, I see, spread out before us, the white sands of Sheepshead Bay. I never knew beaches existed in New York City!

I grab John's elbow. "Look out to the south," I tell him. "There it is!"

"What?" asks John.

"Cuba! It's my Havana! I can just see it!"

"Wow!" says John.

The salty air is as mild as on the Malecón, and the spray coats our arms. New York sunlight, shimmering with the promise of summer, settles around my shoulders like the arms of my mother. It is almost like my Havana.

A Note from the Author

About eight years ago, in 2001, a local radio broadcast featured a five-minute interview with a most interesting Cuban émigré, an architect named Secundino Fernandez. Mr. Fernandez related the story of leaving his beloved home city of Havana with his parents when he was just ten years old. It was in 1959, at the start of the Castro regime. He talked about coming to New York City in the late fifties, which was a much stiffer and less diverse place than it is today, without the large Hispanic community it boasts now.

In the freezing, English-only New York — a black and gray city of ice and howling winds — young Dino felt great homesickness for sun-filled, pastel-hued Havana with its gentle ocean and palm trees. He told of a longing for home so intense that he began to build a cardboard model of Havana on the floor of his bedroom in an effort to alleviate some of his heart's pain.

His story stayed with me for a number of years because it told of the grit that lies inside children, even in the midst of adversity. I, too, had suffered an intense bout of homesickness as a child and will never forget its grip on my heart.

It took me four years to find the real Secundino Fernandez. He was right under my nose on West 16th Street in New York City! I asked for and received his permission and his help in writing this story for young people. Dino flooded me with wonderful memories, old passports, and photo albums, but mostly with beautiful pictures of his dearly beloved Havana, still out of reach for Americans due to the perfidy and silliness of politicians.

Dino Fernandez, age 8, with his parents